MALCOLM ARCHER

INTRADA

MUSIC DEPARTMENT

OXFORD
UNIVERSITY PRESS

for TJS

Intrada

MALCOLM ARCHER

Sw.: Full without 16'
Gt.: 8', 4', 2', Mixture, Sw. to Gt.
Ped.: 16', 8', Reed 16', Gt. to Ped., Sw. to Ped.

© Oxford University Press 2021

Printed in Great Britain

OXFORD UNIVERSITY PRESS, MUSIC DEPARTMENT, GREAT CLARENDON STREET, OXFORD OX2 6DP
The Moral Rights of the Composer have been asserted. Photocopying this copyright material is ILLEGAL.

Allegro ♪ = 240
Ch. 8', 4', Larigot
24
Ch. mp lightly
Ch./Ped. soft 16', 8'
31
37
rall.
Maestoso ♩ = 88
Gt. ff marked
ff
44

51
59
Allegro ♪ = 240
Ch. 8', 4', Larigot
Ch. mp lightly
Ch./Ped. soft 16', 8'
66
72
rall.

Con moto ♩ = 60
77
Gt. (Gt. + Sw. Foundation)
mf
cresc. poco a poco
82
+ Full Sw. (box closed)
88
f
94
Rall.

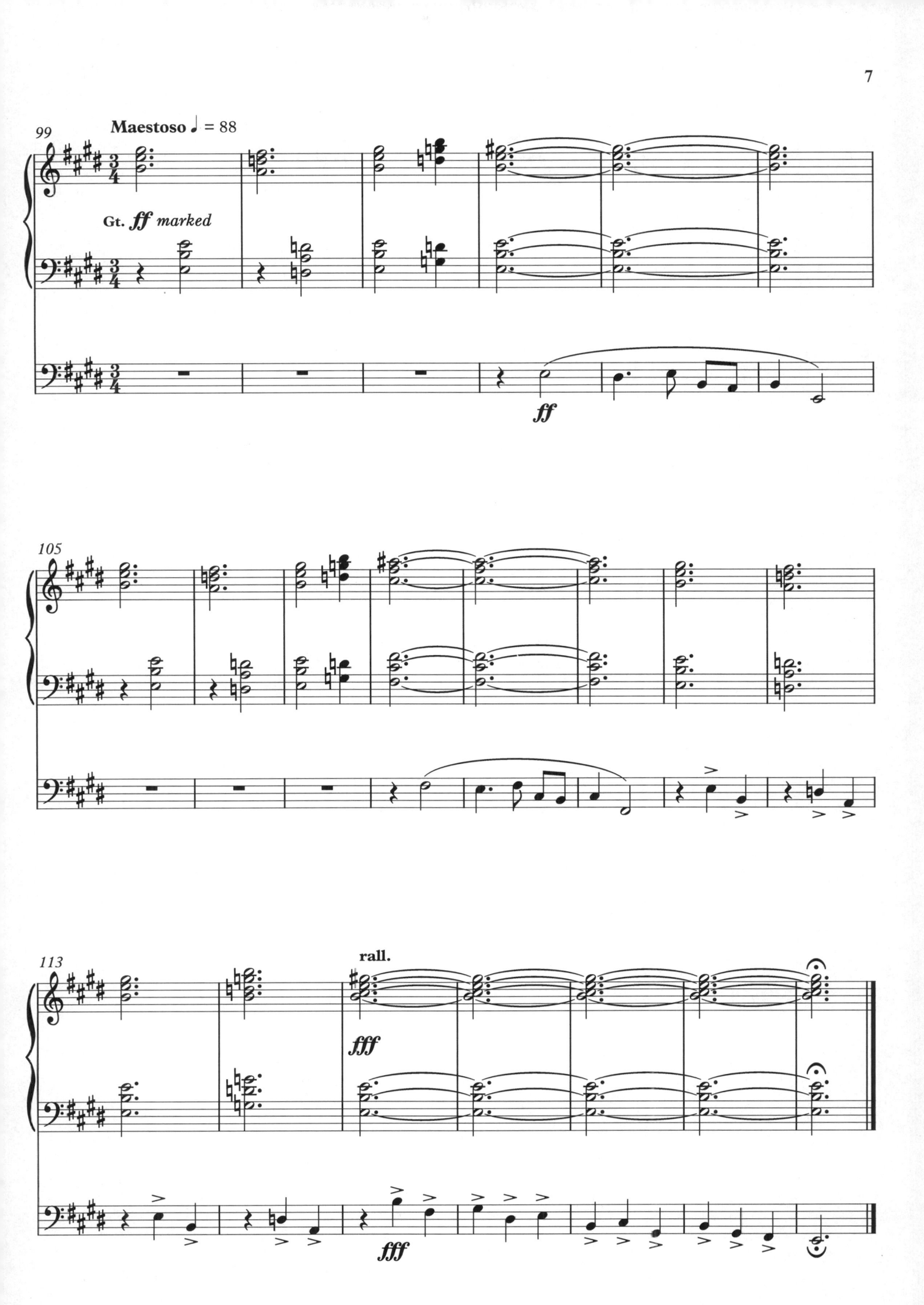
99
Maestoso ♩ = 88
Gt. ff marked
ff
105
113
rall.
fff
fff